Samuel French Acting Edition

Hannah and the Dread Gazebo

by Jiehae Park

SAMUELFRENCH.COM   SAMUELFRENCH.CO.UK

MUSIC USE NOTE

Licensees are solely responsible for obtaining formal written permission from copyright owners to use copyrighted music in the performance of this play and are strongly cautioned to do so. If no such permission is obtained by the licensee, then the licensee must use only original music that the licensee owns and controls. Licensees are solely responsible and liable for all music clearances and shall indemnify the copyright owners of the play(s) and their licensing agent, Samuel French, against any costs, expenses, losses and liabilities arising from the use of music by licensees. Please contact the appropriate music licensing authority in your territory for the rights to any incidental music.

IMPORTANT BILLING AND CREDIT REQUIREMENTS

If you have obtained performance rights to this title, please refer to your licensing agreement for important billing and credit requirements.

HANNAH AND THE DREAD GAZEBO had its world premiere on March 29, 2017, produced by Oregon Shakespeare Festival (Artistic Director, Bill Rauch; Executive Director, Cynthia Rider). The production was directed by Chay Yew, with scenic design by Collette Pollard, costume design by Sara Ryung Clement, and lighting design by David Weiner. The production dramaturg was Lue Douthit and the production stage manager was Gwen Turos. The cast was as follows:

HANNAH / ENSEMBLE. . . . . Cindy Im

FATHER / ENSEMBLE . . . . .Paul Juhn

MOTHER / ENSEMBLE . . . . .Amy Kim Waschke

DANG / ENSEMBLE. . . . . .Sean Jones

GIRL / ENSEMBLE . . . . Eunice Hong

SHAPESHIFTER / ENSEMBLE . . . . Jessica Ko

HANNAH AND THE DREAD GAZEBO was developed at the Ojai Playwrights Conference (Robert Egan, Artistic Director/Producer).

HANNAH AND THE DREAD GAZEBO was developed at the 2013 Bay Area Playwrights Festival, a program of the Playwrights Foundation (Amy L. Mueller, Artistic Director).

CHARACTERS

HANNAH* – (mid-thirties) Doctor. About to become a board-certified pediatric neurologist. Control freak.

FATHER – (fifties) Professor. Keeps it Together for the Family. Emotionally clueless.

MOTHER – (fifties) In a deep depression. Gardening fanatic and HGTV addict.

SHAPESHIFTER / VOICE / GRANDMA / MRS. LEE / OLD MAN IN COAT / OFFICIAL / NURSE / MR. KWON / KIM JONG IL / GRANDMOTHER TIGER

– Trickster-lost-soul-friend-voice-of-god. May or may not have been here since the beginning of the world. Possible memory loss.

DANG* – (early twenties) Recent graduate and professional slacker. Has-a-band-sort-of. Good kid.

GIRL – (twenties) Activist in search of a cause. Used-to-have-a-band-sort-of. Blunt.

*When Mother and Father say Hannah's name, they pronounce it like the Korean name (with no syllabic emphasis: "Hahn-Nah"). Dang pronounces it like the conventional American name: "Hannah." Dang's given name is actually "Dong-euk," but at a certain age he refused to have "Dong" as a first name anymore.

TIME & PLACE

NYC and South Korea
Winter of 2011, just before the death of Kim Jong Il

AUTHOR'S NOTES

Overlaps are indicated by a slash [/].

[Words in brackets] are thought rather than spoken.

(Dialogue in parentheses) is spoken, but indirect.

Placement in parallel columns indicates either overlapping action within scenes or simultaneous scenes in different locations.

There are several "universal gestures" indicated that will help the non-Korean-speaking audience understand what's occurring in Korean language scenes – these gestures should be clean, clear, and uniform among the cast. These gestures will, for the most part, seem intuitive – with one possible exception being the gesture for "North Korea." Past productions have used some variation of pointing to indicate "over there."

Underlined words in Korean (and the English translations) should be lifted vocally, as they are significant/repeated throughout the play. These words often, but not always, correspond to the universal gestures referenced above.

For my family.

PART I. NOW.

(Darkness.)

(The sound of a city at night, far, far below.)

*(A **WOMAN** appears, rushes forward, throws her arms wide open, and disappears.)*

(Darkness.)

HANNAH. This is the story of a wish.

(A small glass bottle with a screw-top appears. A smooth, white stone at the bottom.)

Ordinary enough, right?

(She shakes it. A tiny rattling sound.)

Not a genie, or a magic fish, or a severed monkey's paw – but a 100 percent genuine, bona-fide-heart's-desire-level wish.

Some of you won't believe me. You'd need a piece of paper, a certificate of authenticity like they gave out back when you could buy a piece of the Berlin Wall online. I have one of those too.

(Somewhere else, a fist-sized chunk of the Berlin Wall [with a framed certificate of authenticity] appears – then disappears.)

It came via FedEx, this wish. International Global Express mail from Seoul, Korea. Medium box, not one of those floppy-wax envelopes but a stiff cardboard box and inside that box a wad of bubble wrap and tape and inside that bubble wrap and tape a piece of pink tissue paper with this glass bottle and a suicide note.

*(A **WOMAN** appears, rushes forward, throws her arms wide open, and disappears.)*

HANNAH. It's been in the family for a long time, this wish.

>   *(The small glass bottle disappears.)*

Okay then. Here's how it goes.

>   *(The sound of something fast and heavy [An airplane? Traffic?] approaches, then melts into the sound of wheels spinning, hard.)*

>   *(A man on a bicycle, panting to get up a steep hill. The incline gets suddenly steeper. He pedals harder, meeting it. The bicycle is old, so it's an effort. He climbs higher and higher and – just as he is about to reach the peak – his cell phone rings. He tries to plow forward, but his focus is shattered. It rings again.)*

>   *(He stops, holding the phone as best he can up to his helmeted head.)*

FATHER. 여보세요?

Hi honey! Oh, nothing. You know…"hanging out."

Hmm?

Oh, fine.

How are things?

I'm fine.

Really.

She's fine too. We're all fine.

Why not?

Oh.

Oh that.

She told you huh.

Then how –? Huh. Huh. Okay.

Well, we didn't want you to worry. This is an important time for you.

How is studying going? Two weeks 'til the big day, right?

Yes.

Yes.

Ye– no.

I'm sorry, we didn't want to – yes.

I under–

> *(He looks up at the peak.)*

Are you eating?

Are you exercising?

Are you ever getting married?

Well, make sure you get some exercise. Health is everything. If you don't have your health –

That's true. I guess she doesn't. That's one of the side effects of being dead.

No I'm not trying to be funny, I just – Um. I have a student here, my student's here, honey, Ihavetogo-okloveyoubye.

> *(He puts the phone in his pocket. Looks up the hill and resumes pedaling.)*

HANNAH. There is a videotape, which I will see later, of her on the roof. Wearing only a flimsy nightgown and a pair of pink slippers.

> *(**FATHER** appears, as before, a memory:)*

                             FATHER.
                             How is studying going?
                             Two weeks 'til the big
                             day, right?

HANNAH.

Twelve years of private school.

Four years of college.

Four years of medical school.

Four years of residency.

Four years of neurology fellowship.

Three months of studying and now –

FATHER.
Two weeks 'til the big
day, right?

HANNAH.
Two weeks between
me and the exam to
become a board-certified
pediatric neurologist.

We didn't want you
to worry. This is an
important time for you.

I cannot argue with the
logic of that statement.

See?

(HANNAH looks at FATHER.)

HANNAH. But sometimes logic is bullshit.

*(Unseen, the SHAPESHIFTER slides a suitcase
onstage. HANNAH turns, just missing her but
seeing the suitcase. She picks it up and goes)*

(Shift.)

*(The sound of a television. MOTHER lies on her
side.)*

(The doorbell rings.)

(The doorbell rings.)

(The doorbell rings.)

(She does not respond.)

(The doorbell rings.)

(The doorbell rings.)

(The doorbell –)

(The phone rings.)

*(Without shifting from her horizontal state,
MOTHER brings the phone to her ear. Her voice
is bright.)*

MOTHER. Hello?

Oh hi! No, just watching a little TV. The Garden Channel. I got a trellis last week so I'm researching how to use it. Trellis. Trellis. T-R-E-L – it's like a wall, but for outside. No, no – a normal wall has an inside and an outside but a trellis has an outside and another outside – you hang things from it. Garden-y things.

I know I don't. But I'm going to. And it was free. Anyway, it fits in the living room so I'm going to leave it there for now until we move to a place that –

(Pause.)

But honey it was free.

Craigslist. They have it here too! I went to six different places last week and got free patio furniture, free bricks, someone was giving away a gazebo but I couldn't figure out how to get it back to the apartment. I really wanted that gazebo. I guess it's for the best; it probably wouldn't have fit on the bus.

You know that show in America called *Curb Appeal*? I love that show. That show is the number one thing I miss about living in America. I want my home to have "curb appeal." When people drive by I want them to say, "Ahhhhh, that is the house of a woman who knows how to keep a house." I want the neighbors to grow steamy green with envy that they cannot have such a house. Of course when you live in a high-rise you don't have a curb, so you cannot have Curb Appeal. And people cannot drive by your house, unless they know how to drive in the SKY! Hahahaha! That is very sad. I am sad. I want to die.

Hmm?

Oh, I said, "I want some pie!" I would love a piece of sweet potato pie. No pie here. Cake, yes, cake on every block, but that crust. Sigh. *Pie.*

(The doorbell rings.)

Honey, I have to go, there's someone at the door. Okay. Okay. Okay I love you. Bye.

(She hangs up the phone.)

(She doesn't move.)

(The doorbell rings.)

(She doesn't move.)

(The phone rings. She looks at it, then at the door. Finally, without moving –)

MOTHER. Who is it?

HANNAH. *(A voice through the door.)* It's me Mom.

MOTHER. Oh.

(Beat.)

Oh.

(Shift.)

HANNAH. Every story has a beginning, middle, and end. A leads to B leads to C. Simple.

But human memory is complex – a dynamic cycle of synaptic events reaching, molding, traversing, changing – reshaping the past for the needs of the present to live in the future. "All memories are suspect, at the neural level," my favorite professor says. There's what happened, and what we remember. What we remember, and the story we tell.

(The piece of the Berlin Wall and certificate of authenticity re-appear.)

This piece of paper says that this rock started as part of a wall. Then it got knocked down. Then it got sold for $49.95 plus shipping at www.berlin-wall.net: beginning, middle, end.

But (you might say) what about when the sand was taken from the beach and got poured into concrete, and that concrete hardened to become the wall? Before, we had a story of Destruction! Liberation! The triumph of Internet Capitalism! But before that was a story of Transformation! Separation! A Bigass Wall! It's a question of where you start.

Our story today is a mystery. So for our purposes we'll start –

>   (*A FedEx box drops from the sky and nearly hits* **HANNAH** *on the head.*)

(*Looking up.*) Hey –

VOICE. (*From above.*) Sorry.

HANNAH. Just now, we were approaching the middle. Here is the beginning. Or for you academic types –

>   (*She turns the box, revealing the words "INCITING EVENT." She unwraps a wad of bubble wrap and tape and inside that bubble wrap and tape is a piece of pink tissue paper, and a glass bottle wrapped in a suicide note.*)
>
>   (**HANNAH** *holds up the bottle. Shakes it gently.*)

What the note said, was this:

THE WOMAN. 까치야,
요즘 건강하지? 나, 오늘 밤에 휴전선 남쪽에 있는 "Sunrise Dewdrop Apartment City for Senior Living" 옥상에서 뛰어내릴꺼라, 너에게 이걸 주고싶어. 소원이야. 오~~랫동안 우리 가족에서 전해져 내려온 보물이야.
-할머니가.

HANNAH. And what I understood was *this*:

THE WOMAN. (*In English. Sort of. Where there are ellipses the sound is covered by the "kkccccchhh" of static, like a cheap children's walkie-talkie.*) Little magpie,
I hope you... Tonight I... "Sunrise Dewdrop Apartment City for Senior Living" on... I want you to...this. It is... It...family...long time.
Love,
Grandma.

HANNAH. The next morning I take the note to the dry cleaner one block from my apartment near NYU Medical Center.

(Behind **HANNAH,** *the* **WOMAN (GRANDMA)** *transforms into* **MRS. LEE.***)*

MRS. LEE. When you get this?

HANNAH. Yesterday.

MRS. LEE. Uh-oh.

HANNAH. What does it say?

MRS. LEE. Where your grandma?

HANNAH. Korea.

MRS. LEE. She okay in head?

HANNAH. What do you mean?

MRS. LEE. Crazy lady?

> *(She makes the universal gesture for "crazy lady.")*

HANNAH. Well she has Alzheimer's...my parents moved back to Seoul so my mom could take care of her but they finally had to – whatdoesitsay?

MRS. LEE. You call family.

HANNAH. What does it say?

MRS. LEE. You call now.

HANNAH. What does it say?

MRS. LEE. You have phone?

> *(***HANNAH** *takes out an iPhone.)*

That 4 or 4s?

HANNAH. 4s.

MRS. LEE. You like?

HANNAH. Yeah, it's fine.

MRS. LEE. Okay good you call now.

> *(***HANNAH** *dials.)*

HANNAH. I call my father at the university. No answer.

I call my mother at home. No answer.

I call my brother in Brooklyn. No answer.

I try to call my grandmother at the Sunrise Dewdrop Apartment City for Senior Living but I don't have the phone number. I try to google it, but I do not know how to type "Sunrise Dewdrop Apartment City for Senior Living" in Korean on my keyboard. I google "Korean keyboard."

(She googles "Korean keyboard" on her iPhone 4s. Gah.)

I call my father's cell phone. No answer.

I call my mother's cell phone. No answer.

I sign into my e-mail to send a message to my family to ask WHAT IS GOING ON MOM'S MOM SENT ME THIS NOTE AND MY DRY CLEANER MRS. LEE SAID I NEED TO CALL YOU, when –

(The sound of a guitar chord.)

I notice my brother is "available to chat" on Gmail.

*(**DANG** appears, trying to learn a song online: "G... G... G...")*

	DANG.
	Heeeey.
HANNAH.	
What the hell is going on?	
	Awwwww shit they told you, huh?
Told me what?	
	We didn't want to worry you 'cause'a that big doctor test coming up.
Told me what.	
	Are you sure you wanna know right now? They were gonna call you after you wrapped up all that doctor bizness.
Told. Me. WHAT.	
	...Riiiight... So you know Grandma?

(Silence.)

...So she like, maybe died on Tuesday.

(Beat.)

What.

Yeah...like she kinda jumped off the roof of that retirement home? Like in the middle of the night?

How can you *kinda* jump off a –

Nawww I said that wrong – she jumped – she definitely jumped – but... it's kinda complicated, because she like, jumped onto the wrong side?

Wrong side?

Of the border, right? So they're not allowed to go down and look for her or the soldiers on the other side are allowed to like, shoot and shit. It's a whole other *level* over here.

Where are you?

*(**DANG** plays an awkward guitar chord.)*

HANNAH. And he tells me that he is in Seoul, with my mother and father, and says again that they –

DANG & FATHER. "Didn't want to worry you –

DANG. – Yo."

HANNAH. And I sign off and dial and this time my father picks up *and it sounds like he's in a wind tunnel* but he pretends to have a student waiting for him so he can get off the phone and I book a plane ticket for that night and show up at the front door of their poured concrete high-rise condo 10:30 a.m. local time and I ring but no one answers so I ring again and no one answers so I call and no one answers and I call again and call again and ring again and ring again and I can hear the television behind the door and finally my mother picks up the phone.

MOTHER. Oh.

>   *(Beat.)*

Oh.

HANNAH. And so, for the first time in twenty years, we are all home.

PART II. ARRIVAL.

(Outside. Night. Cold.)

*(**DANG**, in a winter coat. He holds a knit hat in his hands.)*

(He puts the hat on his head, tugs it over his ears.)

DANG. When I get to the city it is like so fuckin' *crowded*, more crowded than anyplace I've ever been and just so full of like *Asian* people, you know? This ocean of skinny people with dark hair and dark eyes and is it racist to notice that and to wish a little bit that they didn't all look like me – like it's messing with my sense of *identity* or whatever, and at the same time it's like they know I don't belong from the way I dress the way I walk the way I *breathe* and I don't really know Grandma I only met her once on Christmas when I was one and peed on her when she picked me up, that's what Dad always says Christmas morning: "Ho ho remember that one time you peed on Grandma," but he doesn't bring it up now and whatever I'm here to support, you know, support Mom and Dad and when I get off the plane the subway the sidewalk in front of their condo there's an old lady beating her chest like this opera I saw on a field trip in ninth grade, 'cept it's *real*, and it's *scary*, and when we get back from that whack high-rise at the border of where people can get shot and it's *legal* I tell Mom and Dad I'm going for a walk and get on the subway and ride it for hours, ride it through CITY and CITY and CITY –

*(**OLD MAN IN COAT** appears.)*

DANG. – 'Til I don't know where I am anymore, and it's just me and this old dude sitting in this subway car alone, and he opens his mouth but I don't understand what he's saying and then all of a sudden –

> *(The* **OLD MAN** *makes a gesture. A flash of light.)*

– I *do*. And maybe I'm hallucinating 'cause I've been on this train so long but I realize this man-on-the-subway-slash-hallucination is telling me a story about the Beginning of the World.

DANG & OLD MAN. A long, long time ago –

DANG. – Before there was a country to have a name, there was a bear, and a tiger. They saw humans – saw how they spoke, and ate, and loved, and like, sung songs and shit, and they wanted more than anything to be like them. To become one of them. So they screwed up their courage and went to the lord of – I don't know what exactly he was lord of, but he was powerful, and back in the day powerful dudes could work some powerful, you know – water into wine and stuff like that. And they said –

"Hey King, we wanna be human. What we gotta do?"

And the king looked at them, and didn't know if they were for real or if they were just like, sayin' stuff without knowin' what it meant.

"Oh yeah?" said the king. "Okay. If you wanna be human, here's what you gotta do. Go live in a cave." A for real cave – dark, dank, stanky, no sunlight, no trees, no contact. No music, no wind, no lakes, no berries, no bougainvillea, no lemons, no ocean no company, no microwave ovens, no shopping malls, no cheesecake or Cheesecake Factory, no super-size, no TV, no internet, no books or coffee or wine or guns or pencils or – did I say light? – Yeah no light, no light at all. Just the dark dark cold and each other and this here *garlic*.

And he hands them these hunks of the foulest, stinkiest, most *bulbous* garlic you ever saw.

A hundred days. If you can stay, if you can manage to not go crazy and not kill each other and make it out the other side cold and hungry and skinny as hell I'll give you enlightenment.

But what about being human?

Yeah, you can have that too.

"*Oh hell no*," thought the bear.

"Okay," said the tiger. "*We got this.*"

So in they go. The whole time the bear is thinking – no way no way on earth am I gonna make it a hundred days with just this stinkass garlic and this tiger and all this dark. But he went along anyway, and they climbed the highest mountain and found the darkest cave and went in in in 'til they couldn't see nothin', nothin' at all. They waited a whole day and said, "Oh that wasn't so bad," and then another day, and on the third day they started to notice that the smell of the garlic wasn't getting any easier to take and man it *was* so bad, and they kept steppin' in piles of their own shit because it was so dark, and the smell of the shit mingled with the smell of the garlic, and it was just garlicky sweaty shitty stink day and night and it was fucking *cold* in that cave so they'd curl up next to each other at night – or at least they thought it was night – for warmth, and wake each other up with their gastrointestinal rumblings and lord the smell *the smell* but every time the bear wanted to run outta there the tiger said, "100. Just 100 days."

So they stayed. And a month went by, and two, and three, and it was so dark they started to forget why they had come to the cave in the first place or that they had faces and voices and anything at all except each other. And on the ninety-first day the tiger had a dream, a scary scary dream that leapt him awake, heard a crash of thunder outside and wondering what it was stumbled out toward the world. And when he got closer to the sunlight leaking into the entrance of the cave his tiger-instincts kicked in and he forgot all about the bear and saw a goat eating a weed on the mountainside and you better believe he pounced on that motherfucker and gobbled him right up. And only then did he remember the bear, and the dream of becoming human, and he let out a *roar* –

> *(The* **OLD MAN** *opens his mouth. The sound of a wild, terrible roar fills the air.)*

– Like you never heard, a tiger-sized roar that shook roots loose and sent rocks tumbling. A roar that scared feathers off birds, and dew off grass, and somewhere deep, deep inside the cave the bear woke up.

DANG & OLD MAN. And saw he was alone.

DANG. And he called out, "Tiger? Tiger? YO YOU ASSWIPE WHERE YOU AT?" And the bear wondered how much time had passed – and ate some garlic, and wondered what in the world was he gonna do? This whole crazy mess wasn't his idea in the first place. He was just a – what *was* he? He couldn't remember anymore. So he stayed inside, and ate some more garlic, and ate some more garlic, and didn't know what to do so ate some *more* garlic. Until one day he heard a voice calling to him – "Hey bear! Bear!" – and it all came back to him and he thought, "Oh shit that's me, I'm Bear and so that must be Tiger," and moved toward it, bumpin' into walls and shit, and walked, and bumped, and bumped, and walked, and there on the ground was a pale, like, *sliver* of light and he moved toward that sliver as it got wider and wider until it became a RIVER of light that poured out of the mouth of the cave and he saw a man standing there. And he was hungry and thought – "I'd like to eat that man, I'd like to eat him right now," but as he stretched out his paw he saw that it was white, and soft, and had no claws, and that *he was a woman*. And his body was small and weak and naked before this man, who looked at him-slash-her and said – "Good work, Bear. *Good work*. And you look *hot*, I mean damn I didn't realize you'd come out so good. I think I'ma marry you."

And the bear looked around for the tiger but he was nowhere to be seen, and here he-slash-she was with no fur and no claws and no clothes and this was clearly a very very powerful dude so did he have a choice?

So he married the king. And that. Is how our country was born.

> *(An announcement in Korean.)*
>
> *(The "ding-dong" of the doors.)*
>
> *(The* **OLD MAN** *turns to go.)*

And I ask him – Yo whattabout that tiger?

> *(The* **OLD MAN** *gestures: "No English.")*

Tiger. *Tiger.* Rrrrar.

> (**DANG** *makes an awkward tiger claw gesture.)*

OLD MAN. *(In recognition.)* Ahhhhhhhhh –

DANG. – He says. Then shrugs.

> *(The* **OLD MAN** *shrugs.)*

– And leaves the subway car.

> *(The* **OLD MAN** *leaves the subway car.)*

And now it's just me and I realize I'm back at the stop where I started, this is my stop, and what must be thirty people come in all at once and the *fuck* did I just dream all this? And then I look out the window and see the back of the little dude moving away from me, and suddenly he turns back at me, and smiles, and opens his coat, and instead of fake watches or gold chains the lining of his coat is strung with garlic. And he like, *winks* at me, and closes his coat, and is gone.

PART III. DINNER.

1.

(The apartment.)

(MOTHER, FATHER, HANNAH, DANG, *and a pie.)*

(Awkward silence. Finally:)

DANG. What kinda pie is this?

HANNAH. Key lime.

(More silence.)

I tried to get sweet potato but they were out.

FATHER. It looks wonderful.

HANNAH. Thanks.

FATHER. Did you make it?

HANNAH. It's Sara Lee.

(Silence.)

Sweet potato is seasonal.

FATHER. Well it looks wonderful.

DANG. I bought one of those once you have to defrost the fuckers like fourteen hours so it was mad smart to take it on the plane with you.

(He tries to cut into it. It's still frozen.)

FATHER. How is the studying going?

HANNAH. Fine.

FATHER. Two weeks 'til the big day, right?

HANNAH. Right.

FATHER. And then would be a good time to make it official with that nice young man, eh?

> *(Pause.)*

Children are life's greatest –

HANNAH. He's going back to Argentina.

DANG. Why?

HANNAH. That's where he's from.

> *(Beat.)*

It's fine.

> *(Silence.)*

MOTHER. Did you see my trellis?

HANNAH. It's very nice.

DANG. What's a trellis.

> (**MOTHER** *points to the trellis.)*

FATHER. I wondered what that was.

MOTHER. It's a wall. But instead of an inside-outside wall, it's an outside-outside wall.

DANG. But we're inside.

FATHER. *("Helpful.")* So it's an inside-inside wall.

> (**MOTHER** *looks at* **FATHER**.*)*

MOTHER. There was a gazebo, but it wouldn't fit on the bus.

FATHER. That's too bad.

DANG. Where would you put a gazebo?

> *(They all stare at the pie.)*

HANNAH. How's the band?

DANG. We're taking a break.

FATHER. Again?

DANG. Stacey got a job in Portland so we're lookin' for a new bass-slash-mandolin player. And Gay Bob is doing this pre-med bizness at Columbia.

HANNAH. Gay Bob?

DANG. It's his legal name.

HANNAH. No one's legal name is Gay Bob.

DANG. He changed it.

FATHER. So that leaves –

HANNAH. Just you.

DANG. Temporary, yo. Temporary.

MOTHER. I really wanted that gazebo.

>*(They look at her.)*

It was free.

>**(HANNAH***'s phone rings.)*
>*(She looks at the caller ID and hits "ignore.")*

FATHER. Who was that?

HANNAH. No one.

>**(HANNAH***'s phone rings again.)*
>*(She hits "ignore" again.)*

Why is there a retirement home –

FATHER. Apartment City for Senior Living.

HANNAH. – Apartment – fine – on the border of the DMZ?

FATHER. They built one on the other side.

>*(He makes the universal gesture for "over there in North Korea.")*

HANNAH. In North Korea?

FATHER. 김정일's orders. To show how well off they are, which is silly, because people are starving over there, everyone knows that –

DANG. I saw some CNN shit 'bout that, buildings with *no glass* in the windows –

FATHER. Propaganda. And even though *we* know that they're only pretending it's better over *there*, our side put something up to make sure *they* know it's really better over *here*.

HANNAH. Who?

DANG. The Communists, Han.

FATHER. The government built a retirement home on the border to show *we* take care of our old people, unlike *their* side, where people probably don't even get old because they're so poor and even if they did they'd probably eat their old people.

> *(**HANNAH** looks at him.)*

Because everyone's so hungry.

HANNAH. I don't think they eat their old people.

FATHER. *(Darkly.)* You never know, with Communists.

They've even dug *secret tunnels* under the border, we've found a few, sure, but who knows how many more are out there?

DANG. Commies be like –

> *(He makes the wriggling, universal gesture for "invade across the border under secret underground tunnels.")*
>
> *(He makes it again, for an "invasion" through a different tunnel.)*
>
> *(And again.)*

As we *speak.*

FATHER. Gratitude is scientifically proven to increase longevity. Your grandmother came from the North, fled South before the ceasefire in '53, so we thought it might be nice for her to be able to look at the other side and see how much better off she was over here.

HANNAH. At the Sunrise Dewdrop –

FATHER. – Apartment City for Senior Living. Right.

MOTHER. She hated it there.

FATHER. Why would you think that?

MOTHER. She said, "I hate it here."

FATHER. She was probably having a bad day.

MOTHER. She said it every day.

FATHER. Let's not get into this now.

DANG. It was prolly the smell.

(To **HANNAH.***)* Old-people funky funk.

HANNAH. So, the problem is...

FATHER. One side of the building butts up against a forest that if we try to enter there's maaaaaybe the potential to trigger a major international incident.

DANG. Also the landmines.

FATHER. Right.

DANG. *(To* **HANNAH.***)* There are landmines.

FATHER. We heard you.

DANG. – And endangered species, like a billion different species' 'cause there's no people they're just hangin' out – like, "Yo, I'm an endangered scarlet-billed plumpy-bird, just me and my buddy the endangered dot-bellied brown bear and these here landmines," which makes you wonder, it would be crazy, right, if there's just like one of these scarlet-billed plumpy-birds in the world, just one, and nobody knows about it, and it plops down on a landmine and BOOOOM.

> *(He makes the universal gesture for "landmines-then-boom.")*

FATHER. Anyway, we've sent a request through the proper diplomatic channels, and until then –

DANG. We're waitin' for the Communists to give us permission to look for Grandma's body.

FATHER. We don't know she's dead.

DANG. Uh –

FATHER. We don't know she's dead.

HANNAH. When will they give us an answer?

MOTHER. I don't feel well.

> *(She exits.)*

> *(***HANNAH*** looks at* **DANG.***)*

HANNAH. Do you have to / talk about landmines and exploding birds?

FATHER. She'll be fine.

Grandma wasn't herself, near the... It's been hard.

(Beat.)

HANNAH. Grandma sent me something. Before –

(She takes the note out of her pocket and shows **FATHER***. He reads.)*

What does it say?

FATHER. *(Handing back the note.)* It's nonsense. Grandma was physically there, but mentally...she didn't even recognize your mother anymore.

HANNAH. Why didn't you tell me it was that bad?

FATHER. Don't show that to your mother.

HANNAH. How can I help?

*(***FATHER*** shakes his head – he'll take care of it.)*

FATHER. I have an appointment tomorrow – Undersecretary Kwon of the Department of Defense. We'll know more then.

(He exits. **DANG** *and* **HANNAH** *stare at the pie.)*

2.

(**FATHER** *waits in the lobby of the Undersecretary of Defense, carrying his bicycle helmet. The* **OFFICIAL SECRETARY TO THE UNDERSECRETARY OF DEFENSE** *enters – he is very important and very busy.*)

[The following scene is entirely in Korean. Words that are <u>underlined</u> correspond to specific physical gestures that are repeated whenever those underlined words recur throughout the play.]

OFFICIAL. [Yes?]
예! 무슨일입니까?

FATHER. [I'm here to see <u>Mr. Kwon.</u>]
<u>권선생</u> 만날려고 왔습니다.

OFFICIAL. [Do you have an appointment?]
시간예약을 하셨습니까?

FATHER. [Yes. I'm here about my mother-in-law's body?]
예. 장모님 시신때문에 왔습니다.

OFFICIAL. [Eh?]
예?

FATHER. [I was told to come here this morning (about her body in) <u>North Korea</u> –]
오늘 아침에 오면 <u>북한</u>에 있는 –

OFFICIAL. [*<u>North Korea</u>?!* What about <u>North Korea</u>?]
<u>북한</u>*?!* <u>북한</u>이 어쨌다고~?

FATHER. [Well not in <u>North Korea</u> technically...]
따질려면 <u>북한</u>은 아니지만...

OFFICIAL. [What do you know about <u>North Korea</u>?]
<u>북한</u>에 대해서 뭘 아십니까?

FATHER. [No, no, she jumped off a <u>roof</u> into the DMZ –]
그게 아니고, <u>옥상</u>에서 비무장지대로 / 뛰어내려서

OFFICIAL. (*Making the universal gesture for "crazy lady":*)
[Ahhhh that <u>crazy woman</u>. "Sunrise –"]
아~그 <u>미친년</u> 얘기구나. "Sunrise –"

FATHER & OFFICIAL. – "Dewdrop Apartment City for Senior Living."

> (*The* **OFFICIAL** *makes the universal gesture for "jump off a tall building."*)

FATHER. [Right.]
예.

OFFICIAL. [Haven't you heard the news? About *Kim Jong Il*?]
소식 못들으셨습니까? 김정일에 대해서?

FATHER. [*Kim Jong Il?*]
김정일?

> (*The* **OFFICIAL** *makes the universal across-the-neck gesture for "dead."*)

OFFICIAL. [It's been pandemonium here! Come back tomorrow.]
여기 지금 난장판이에요! 내일 돌아오십시오.

> (*The* **OFFICIAL** *bows and turns to go.*)

FATHER. [But –]
하지만 –

> (*The* **OFFICIAL** *has a thought and turns back.*)

OFFICIAL. [That was very unpatriotic of her. How will that look to the starving Communists?]
그여자 참 애국심이 없구만. 굶어죽는 빨갱이들이 우릴 어떻게 생각하겠소?

> (*The* **OFFICIAL** *exits.* **FATHER** *turns and walks into...*)

3.

*(**DANG** and **HANNAH** are watching the news. Sounds of rapid-fire Korean commentary, with the name "Kim Jong Il" repeated over and over again.)*

DANG. Does this, um, affect stuff over here?

FATHER. I have to go back tomorrow.

DANG. No, like other stuff.

HANNAH. He means –

DANG. – Are we gonna get nuked?

FATHER. Of course not.

DANG. How do you know?

*(**FATHER** shrugs.)*

FATHER. Hasn't happened yet!

DANG. *(Squinting at the screen.)* They're all wearing the same red pin. What is it?

HANNAH. Buttons. With his face.

DANG. Creepy.

FATHER. Communist.

Where's your mother?

HANNAH. She was just here.

DANG. Maybe she went out?

FATHER. *(Alarmed.)* Did you show her that note?

HANNAH. No.

FATHER. *(Relieved.)* Good.

*(**HANNAH** looks at him, suspicious.)*

(Backpedaling.) It's nonsense.

*(**HANNAH** takes out the note again.)*

HANNAH. What does it say?

FATHER. I told you, it's non–

HANNAH. But what –

FATHER. Your grandma wasn't herself.

DANG. Yeah, she jumped off a *roof*.

FATHER. Allegedly.

DANG. Isn't there, like, video?

> (*The first moment of the play recurs, but from the reverse perspective. A* **WOMAN** *runs away from us, throws her arms forward, and disappears.*)

HANNAH. There's video?

DANG. Military cameras, Han.

FATHER. Not of everything – the actual jumping, no.

DANG. But she only runs in the one direction.

FATHER. So?

DANG. Did she, like, *fly* off the sixty-third floor?

HANNAH. Dad, just.

Tell me.

> (**FATHER** *sighs. Takes it and reads.*)

FATHER.

(*In English.*) Little magpie,
I hope you are doing well. Tonight I am going to jump off the roof of the Sunrise Dewdrop Apartment City for Senior Living on the south-side border of the Demilitarized Zone, so I want you to have this. It is a wish. It has been in the family for a long time.
Love,
Grandma.

GRANDMA.

(*In Korean, simultaneous.*) 까치야,
요즘 건강하지? 나, 오늘 밤에 휴전선 남쪽에 있는 "Sunrise Dewdrop Apartment City for Senior Living"옥상에서 뛰어내릴꺼라, 너에게 이걸 주고싶어. 소원이야. 오~~랫 동안 우리 가족에서 전해져 내려온 보물이야.

– 할머니가.

DANG. Guess that answers that question.

> (**HANNAH** *removes the bottle from her pocket.*)

HANNAH. This was in the box.

FATHER. What is it?

HANNAH. I don't know

FATHER. A rock?

HANNAH. It's so white – like bone.

DANG. "A wish" – what does that mean?

HANNAH. *(To* **FATHER.***)* Do you know?

FATHER. No clue.

HANNAH. Maybe I should ask Mom.

FATHER. Don't bother her with –

DANG. You think it could be real?

HANNAH. Real what?

DANG. You know, a *wi*–

      *(***HANNAH*** snorts.)*

HANNAH. Like a genie?

DANG. I dunno.

      *(***HANNAH*** and* **FATHER** *look at him, incredulous.)*

  (Defensive.) It's weird here.

FATHER. It's not weird.

DANG. (Nevermind.)

HANNAH. Why'd she send it to me?

DANG. 'Cause she was –?

      (He makes the universal sign for "crazy lady.")

FATHER. *Dang.*

HANNAH. Maybe Mom [would know] –

FATHER. Do not mention this to –

HANNAH. But –

      *(***MOTHER*** enters.* **FATHER** *hides the note.* **HANNAH** *hides the bottle.)*

MOTHER. What's the limit on the Mastercard?

FATHER. Six million Won? Seven?

(She exits.)

HANNAH. She might / know.

FATHER. Not now.

HANNAH. She has a right to / know.

FATHER. Not now.

(Beat.)

HANNAH. Can I see the video?

FATHER. Kind of morbid, don't you think?

DANG. Yeah it's dark so you can't see that much anyway.

FATHER. *(Explaining.)* He's a boy.

DANG. Men handle this kind of thing better.

FATHER. You have to concentrate on your studies. Don't they only offer this test once a year?

HANNAH. I'll make it.

FATHER. This is an important time for you.

(He takes his helmet and exits. They hear the door squeak, then close. The ding of the elevator.)

*(**DANG** and **HANNAH** stand there, silence broken only by the newscasters' voices and the sounds of very loud, very public mourning.)*

*(**DANG** looks again at the glass-bottled wish.)*

DANG. It's pretty.

HANNAH. I guess.

DANG. Can I hold it?

HANNAH. No.

(Shift.)

*(**HANNAH** looks at the note again.)*

"...The Sunrise Dewdrop Apartment City for Senior Living..."

(Shift.)

4.

*(A **NURSE** is deeply buried in a fashion magazine at the front desk of the Sunrise Dewdrop Apartment City for Senior Living. Muzak. The hum of fluorescent lights. That vibe belonging almost exclusively to Places for the Very Old and Very Young – the vibe that says, "Our staff is friendly and nonthreatening," and, "Our corners are padded and un-cornerlike." There is a construction-paper rainbow at the front desk and at the end of that rainbow is a bedpan full of lollipops.)*

*(**HANNAH** enters. Sniffs the air [old-people funky funk]. Ignores it as best she can.)*

HANNAH. Hi.

*(The **NURSE** does not look up.)*

Excuse me?
Hello?

*(**HANNAH** taps on the counter. The **NURSE** wakes up.)*

NURSE. *(In Korean.)* [EEE!]
아 깜짝이야!

HANNAH. AGH!

NURSE. [Christ you scared me!]
아 진짜! 놀랐잖아요!

HANNAH. God you scared me.

(Beat.)

NURSE. [Can I help you…?]
도와드릴일 있나요?

HANNAH. Uhh…English?

NURSE. *(In English.)* No.

HANNAH. Really?

NURSE. *(Deadpan.)* Rlee-uh-lee.

HANNAH. Is there anyone else around?

> *(Trying to communicate in terrible, created-in-the-moment hand signals:)*

"Anyone..." "Else..." "aROUND"?

NURSE. [You come to my country and expect me to understand your language?]
남의 나라에 와가지고 지 하는말 알아 들으라는 거야?

HANNAH. My parents only spoke English to us growing up so we'd –

> *(Making a big circle with her arms:)*

A-ROUNNNNND?

NURSE. [No one but me. Deal.]
나 말고 없어. 어쩔건대?

HANNAH. *(Pointing up.)* Can you take me to the roof?

NURSE. [Why are you talking to me like a retarded person?]
내가 등신이냐? 왜 그렇게 말하는거야?

HANNAH. ROOF?

NURSE. *(Making the universal sign for "roof.")* [The *roof*?]
옥상?

HANNAH. *(Making the universal sign for each of the following words.)* ROOF!! OLD WOMAN? JUMPED?

NURSE. *(Making the universal sign for "crazy lady" and "roof.")* [Ohhhh you mean the *crazy lady* who jumped. You want to see the *roof*? That's morbid.]
아~ 자살한 그 미친년 말하는구나~. 옥상을 보고싶다고? 제 정신이 아니구만.

HANNAH. *(Still gesturing.)* OLD WOMAN? JUMP AND POOF?

> *(The **NURSE** stares at her. Puts a key on the counter and points in the direction of the roof. **HANNAH** takes the key and starts to go. Turns and reaches for a lollipop. The **NURSE** slaps her hand away.)*

Ow!

NURSE. [Residents only. Don't get shot.]
거주자만 가져갈수 있어. 총알 조심해.

HANNAH. What?

> (*The* **NURSE** *mimes someone aiming a gun and someone else getting shot, then indicates that would be a bad idea. Then smiles and points to the stairwell.*)

5.

> (**MOTHER** *tends to her trellis. A single vine with heart-shaped leaves winds up from a small pot.*)
>
> (**FATHER** *enters with a credit card statement.*)

FATHER. Did anyone order something for 6,400,000 Won from a company called "Amish Country Gazebos"?

> *(Beat.)*

Anyone?

MOTHER. Do you see a gazebo in this apartment?

FATHER. No...

MOTHER. Okay then.

> *(Beat.)*

FATHER. But –

MOTHER. Where would I put a gazebo?

FATHER. Right.

6.

(The roof. Chilly. The flutter of a bird overhead.)

*(**HANNAH** approaches the edge. She looks down. Faint sounds of the forest far below.)*

(Arms outstretched, she closes her eyes.)

(She takes out the bottled wish and holds it up to the light.)

HANNAH. What are you?

(Far off – but it doesn't sound all that far – someone fires a warning shot.)

*(Startled, **HANNAH** quickly backs away from the edge.)*

7.

(A subway platform. **DANG** *waits for the train. A* **GIRL** *hands out fliers, unsuccessfully.)*

GIRL. *(In really bad Korean. Really bad.)* [Peace our park! Peace our park! Force un-landmine UNESCO Peace Park!]

Pyung-hwa oolli kung won! Pyung-hwa oolli kung won! Jie-lwey up-suh man-dull-o-UNESCO Peace Park!

> *(***DANG*** *looks up. She catches his eye. He suddenly becomes very interested in the Velcro on his left sneaker. She pushes a brochure in front of him.)*

[Peace our park! UNESCO! Park!]

Pyung-hwa oolli kung won! UNESCO! Park!

DANG. Sorry, I –

GIRL. *(In perfect English.)* Oh you're American!

> *(She pushes the brochure toward him again.)*

Can you vote?

DANG. You mean here?

GIRL. Yes!

DANG. Sorry.

GIRL. *(Dejected.)* Oh.

> *(She turns to pursue someone else. Then turns back.)*

I know you. How do I know you?

DANG. I don't think you know me.

GIRL. Where are you from?

DANG. You prolly have me confused with somebody else. *(A joke.)* We all kinda look the same here.

GIRL. *(A fact.)* That's racist.

DANG. Uh.

GIRL. Just 'cause you're Asian doesn't make you not racist.

(She looks at his t-shirt.)

Wait – are you in New Tastier Glaze?

DANG. You know New Tastier Glaze?

GIRL. My bass player sent me a link to your YouTube video last summer. The one in the Laundromat?

DANG. You saw that? Like four people saw that.

GIRL. We used it in *our* YouTube video set in a Laundromat.

DANG. Are you in a band?

GIRL. Was.

DANG. What happened?

*(**GIRL** shrugs.)*

GIRL. I needed to do something that mattered to people other than me and my upper-middle-class overeducated peer group. Are you on tour?

DANG. Family.

GIRL. Your family's here? Can they vote?

DANG. I think so?

*(**GIRL** pushes a brochure at him.)*

GIRL. There's a referendum coming up to ratify the UN resolution to designate a portion of the Demilitarized Zone a UNESCO Biosphere Reserve and remove the one-point-three million landmines / that –

DANG. Yeah I saw some CNN / shit 'bout that –

GIRL. *(Plowing over him.)* Forests in South Korea are at less than five percent of 1910 levels, but the *DMZ* can still be saved –

DANG. Yeah / I saw –

GIRL. *(Still plowing.)* The endangered species there *need* our protection – the Asiatic black bear, the Amur leopard, maybe even white Siberian *tigers* –

(He looks at her – tigers?)

This is a long-range photo of a wild boar whose rear legs were blown off by landmines. Isn't it cute? And angering? / We have to protect –

DANG. Yeah, remember / when I said –

GIRL. Great so you'll talk to your parents?

DANG. Yeah, I guess. Okay.

Why'dju make a video in a Laundromat of my band's video in a Laundromat?

GIRL. It was a commentary on our generation's embrace of new media as a desperate but ultimately futile attempt to create meaning through the gaze of an imaginary secular "Other." No offense.

DANG. None taken.

GIRL. Great.

DANG. 'Cause I don't really understand what you said?

GIRL. Also I was relating my own personal narrative to prove that even when you recognize that need, it doesn't make it any less desperate or futile. Just ironic. Which is death. Because in an age of total media saturation you can't watch the watcher without awareness of being both watcher and watched yourself. It's borderline hopeless.

And my dad had a Laundromat.

DANG. Who's racist now?

GIRL. That doesn't make me racist, that makes me a stereotype. Anyway, he doesn't have it anymore because we live here now.

    (Beat.)

What happened to your band?

DANG. We're on hiatus.

GIRL. You broke up?

DANG. It's temporary.

GIRL. You totally broke up. That's why you look so sad.

DANG. No –

GIRL. You're wearing a t-shirt for your own band that no longer exists in a foreign country where you don't speak the language. I think you've proved my point.

DANG. What point?

GIRL. About the tragi-comic futility of staking a narrative identity claim / on –

DANG. Was this like a *school* band?

(*Sound of the train approaching the station.*)

I gotta go.

(*A subway announcement in Korean as the doors open.*)

(**DANG** *steps onto the train. As the doors close:*)

GIRL. Don't forget to give your parents the brochure. Referendum in nine days!

8.

(FATHER waits in the lobby of the Undersecretary of Defense.)

(The following scene is entirely in Korean.)

OFFICIAL. [Yes?]
예! 무슨일입니까?

FATHER. [Mr. Kwon – *North Korea?*]
권선생 – 북한?

OFFICIAL. [*North Korea?!* What about *North Korea?*]
북한?! 북한이 어쨌다고~?

FATHER. *(Making the universal sign for "roof.")* [My mother-in-law's body...*the roof* –]
장모님의시신...옥상에서 –

> *(FATHER makes the universal gesture for "jump off a roof.")*

OFFICIAL. [Do you have any idea the kind of strain we're under? There's no telling what they're up to now that *Kim Jong Il* is
우리 지금 얼마나 바쁜지 아십니까? 지금 무슨일을 할지 모른다고! 김정일이 –

> *(The OFFICIAL makes the universal across-the-neck gesture for "dead.")*

[– *nuclear weapons* –]
– 핵무기 –

> *(He makes the universal gesture for "nuclear mushroom cloud.")*

[– *tunnels* under the DMZ –]
– 땅굴 –

> *(He makes the universal gesture for "secret underground tunnels.")*

[Come back tomorrow.]
내일 다시 오십시오.

FATHER. [But –]
하지만 –

OFFICIAL. [That's right Goodbye.]
예~! 안녕히 가쇼~

> (The **OFFICIAL** bows and exits. **FATHER** puts on
> his bicycle helmet and turns to face:)

9.

*(**MOTHER, HANNAH,** and **DANG** wait at home.)*

FATHER. Good news or bad news?

DANG. / Good.

HANNAH. Bad.

FATHER. Well, there's still no answer.

HANNAH. And?

FATHER. And what?

DANG. And what's the good news?

FATHER. That's it.

HANNAH. Then what's the bad news?

FATHER. That's it too.

HANNAH. Dad.

FATHER. As long as we can't get permission to go look we don't know if she's dead or if she's not dead. So that's good news, but it's also bad news.

HANNAH. And no news.

DANG. And no body.

MOTHER. Maybe I should –

FATHER. I'm going back tomorrow.

MOTHER. When will we find her?

FATHER. Soon.

DANG. Assuming there's something left to find, right?

FATHER. Dang.

DANG. What there's like bears and *tigers* and shit –

FATHER. / Dang –

DANG. Whole area is a wild animal park but with like, mines. I met this girl who – damn I was supposed to give you that brochure –

    (He exits.)

FATHER. *(To **MOTHER**.)* We don't know she's dead.

HANNAH. Dad.

FATHER. *(To* **HANNAH.***)* We don't –

HANNAH. *(To* **FATHER.***)* You have to tell her –

MOTHER. Tell me what?

FATHER. Not now.

MOTHER. Tell me what?

HANNAH. Mom, Grandma –

> (**HANNAH** *takes out the note;* **FATHER** *unsuccessfully tries to grab it as* **HANNAH** *dodges.)*

FATHER. *(Still reaching.)* Hannah.

HANNAH. *(Still dodging.) Grandma sent me this note.*

> (**MOTHER** *grabs the note.)*

FATHER. *(To* **MOTHER,** *in Korean.)* [Dear –]
    당신 –

> (**MOTHER** *reads.)*

> (**DANG** *re-enters, waving a brochure.)*

DANG. Found it!

> (He sees what's happening in the room – freezes.)

FATHER. *(To* **MOTHER,** *gentle.)* She wasn't well.

DANG. Mom?

> (**HANNAH** *takes the bottle out of her pocket.)*

HANNAH. Do you know what this is?

> (**MOTHER** *takes the bottle, looks at it.)*

MOTHER. She sent it to you?

HANNAH. What is it?

> (**MOTHER** *shakes the bottle gently. A tiny rattling sound.)*

MOTHER. It was for me.

HANNAH. For you? Then why would she –

> (**MOTHER** *hands it back to* **HANNAH.***)*

MOTHER. I'm going up to my gazebo.

> (**MOTHER** *exits.*)

HANNAH. Up?

FATHER. What gazebo?

> (*Beat.*)

> (*To* **DANG** *and* **HANNAH.**) She'll be fine.

>> (**MOTHER** *re-enters.*)

See?

> (**MOTHER** *takes the bottle from* **HANNAH.**)

HANNAH. Mom –

> (**MOTHER** *exits.*)

FATHER. She just needs a minute. To process.

> (*The front door squeaks, then closes. A ding.*)

DANG. Was that the elevator?

HANNAH. (*Realizing.*) The roof.

DANG. Should we –?

FATHER. (*Realizing.*) Ohhhhhh that's where she put the – [gazebo] –

HANNAH. *Dad.*

FATHER. What?

DANG. *The roof.*

FATHER. Oh.

> (*Beat.*)

Oh.

> (*They run.*)

> (*As somewhere else,* **MOTHER** *runs forward, arms outstretched, and leaps into –*)

> (*Darkness.*)

PART IV. THE MIDDLE.

(The phone rings.)
(The phone rings.)
(The phone rings.)

HANNAH. I met this woman. In the elevator, NYU Medical Center. Thirty-eight, postdoctoral researcher at Columbia, fresh out of the hospital where she had been treated for a Type-3 brain aneurysm that caused a seizure that caused a fall that caused a concussion that caused an MRI that finally, accidentally caused her doctors to find the benign tumor exerting pressure on her limbic system that had caused the deep deep depression that had always made her think there was something wrong with her head, caused her to exclaim on rainy days that there was something wrong with her head she was so unhappy this wasn't normal, causing her mother and father to send her to sympathetic-eyed psychiatrists who prescribed Prozac and Zoloft and a long list of hard-to-pronounce SSRIs that caused her despair for not fixing the pounding the feeling that something was *wrong with her head* until finally she gave up and decided to fuck it just live with the pounding the pounding that must be the way that everyone felt they just never talked about it at least she had five fingers on each hand and five toes on each foot and the sun in the morning and the moon at night.
So yeah, they found this tumor. And she was healed.

(The phone rings.)
(The phone rings.)
(The phone rings.)

HANNAH. It has been seven hours, twenty-three minutes, and fourteen seconds since Mom took the elevator up to the roof.

　　(Beat.)

The hospital.

1a.

(The hospital. Noise. A lot of noise.)

FATHER. Where are they where are they where are they?

DANG. Relax, yo. Said she'd be back in a minute.

FATHER. I don't know why we aren't allowed to stay in the room with her, don't you think it's stupid that we're not allowed to –

DANG. Dad. Dude.

FATHER. – There must be someone who can –

DANG. Dude.

HANNAH. Dad.

> *(A **NURSE** enters. She looks an awful lot like the nurse from the Sunrise Dewdrop Apartment City for Senior Living.)*

Hey!

NURSE. *(Coolly, professionally, and in Korean.)* [Yes? How can I help you?]
예~~? 어떻게 도와 드릴까요?

HANNAH. Oh, sorry... I thought you were someone else.

FATHER. [Pardon my daughter she thoughtyouwere someoneelse whereis*mywife* / SOMEONE NEEDS TO TELL US SOMETHING!]
죄송합니다. 제   딸이   다른사함인줄았습니다
아내는갔습니까 / 누군가가 대답좀 해줘요!

NURSE. [I'm sorry sir, but you're going to have to calm down.]
손님, 진정하십시오.

DANG. Dad.

FATHER. I KNOW.

NURSE. [Sir, you're going to have to calm down.]
손님, 진정하셔야만 합니다.

HANNAH. Dad –

FATHER. Fine, *fine.* I'm fine. See?

(The **NURSE** *looks at her clipboard.)*

NURSE. [Are you the *Lees*?]
혹시 이씨 가족입니까?

FATHER. [Yes! The *Lees*!]
예! 이씨 가족입니다.

(The **NURSE** *looks down at her clipboard.)*

NURSE. [I'm sorry to inform you that your mother is dead.]
죄송하지만, 어머니는 돌아가셨습니다.

FATHER. [Dead?]
죽.었.다.고?

(The **NURSE** *makes the universal across-the-neck gesture for "dead.")*

NURSE. [Please fill out this paperwork.]
이 서류들 작성해 주십시오.

(She pushes the clipboard toward **FATHER**.*)*

DANG. What's going on?

HANNAH. What is she saying?

FATHER. Your mother is...

(He looks down at the clipboard.)

...not eighty-three years old.
(To the **NURSE**.*)* This is not my wife.

(She looks at him, puzzled. He repeats, this time in Korean:)

[This is not my *wife*!]
이분은 제 아내가 아닙니다!

(The **NURSE** *takes the clipboard.)*

NURSE. [What's your name?]
성함이 뭐죠?

FATHER. *(Pointing to himself.)* [*Lee* – Ho-sun *Lee*.]
이 – 이.호.선.

NURSE. [Oops!]
앗!

(She calls offstage:)

[Lee Bo-sun? Mr. Lee Bo-sun?]
이.보.선? 이보선 선생님?

1b.

(Somewhere along the 250-kilometer stretch of land known as the Demilitarized Zone. Lush. Wild.)

MOTHER. Am I dead? Is this what dead feels like?

(She bends down to pick a flower.)

(A strange animal, part weasel, part rabbit, hops up to her.)

Hello Mr. Rabbit.

(She pets it.)

Are we dead?

(It hops away.)

Where are you going? Do you want me to follow you?

(An explosion.)

(An object arcs onstage and lands in front of her.)

(She picks up the object. It is a severed rabbit's foot.)

That's ironic.

Was that a landmine? Where could I be where there are...

(She freezes.)

Oh.

(Somewhere, off, the roar *of a large animal. Tiger? Bear?)*

*(*Roar.*)*

That doesn't sound very friendly.

1c.

(The hospital. **HANNAH**, **DANG**, *and* **FATHER**, *still seated.)*

*(***FATHER*** *holds a magazine from the waiting room.)*

FATHER. Here is the plan.

DANG. What?

FATHER. Yes?

HANNAH. What's the plan?

FATHER. I was hoping if I began with that sentence, the middle and end would follow.

(Explaining.) There's this famous German man who tried to commit suicide but it didn't work so he found god and now he's a famous life coach. He says if you state what you want as if it already happened, it will happen.

Here is the plan.

(Beat.)

HANNAH. Did you just read about this in that magazine?

FATHER. Do you have another suggestion?

(Beat.)

DANG. Here is the plan.

(Beat.)

FATHER. She will wake up any minute now.

(Beat.)

HANNAH. She will wake up any minute now.

(Beat.)

FATHER. She's going to be fine.

HANNAH. She is going to be fine.

DANG. That nurse will come back and tell us she is fine.

(They turn around.)

(The **NURSE** *walks by. Completely by. And exits.)*

DANG. / I'm going for a walk

FATHER. Call me if anything changes.

*(***DANG** *and* **FATHER** *exit, in opposite directions.)*

(Shift.)

*(***HANNAH** *holds up the bottled wish.)*

HANNAH. "It's a wish," she said.

*(***MOTHER** *appears, a memory. They look at each other.)*

MOTHER. It was for me.

(She takes the bottle from **HANNAH***.)*

(The ding of an elevator.)

*(***GRANDMA** *appears, a memory.)*

GRANDMA. It's been in the family for a long time.

(Ding.)

(As before, **MOTHER** *rushes forward, her arms wide open –)*

(But this time, instead of darkness, we see her trip.)

(She does a slow-motion face-plant in the cement and passes out.)

(The bottle rolls out of her hand onto the rooftop.)

*(***HANNAH** *picks up the bottle.)*

HANNAH. Beginning, middle –

2.

(The subway. **DANG** *is seated.)*

(Ding-dong.)

*(***GIRL*** *enters.)*

DANG. Hey.

*(***GIRL*** *looks at him.)*

It's me, remember? Sad own-band-t-shirt-guy?

*(***GIRL*** *signals "No English" and "I don't know what you're talking about.")*

(He feels really bad. And really racist. He starts to almost-cry-but-not.)

Goddamnit.

(Beat.)

GIRL. Ha, just fucking with you.

*(***DANG*** *looks at her.)*

DANG. You really suck at being, like, a relatable human being.

GIRL. I have Asperger's.

(A beat, in which **DANG** *has no idea what to say or how to apologize.)*

Just kidding. Koreans don't believe in autism.

(Beat.)

You look extra sad today, sad own-band-t-shirt-guy.

(Beat.)

DANG. My grandma sent a suicide note to my sister in New York before jumping off the roof of her retirement home into the DMZ and two nights ago my mom saw the note, went up to the roof and tried to jump but tripped and she should be fine but she's not waking up and I've been riding this train for hours and oh yeah there's also this bottle with maybe a magical wish inside. Or a rock.

(Beat.)

GIRL. What are you going to do?

DANG. You don't think I'm crazy?

GIRL. *(Shrugging.)* What are you going to *do*?

DANG. I'm waiting.

GIRL. For?

DANG. A man. In a trench coat. With garlic in his pockets.

GIRL. Is that code for some weird sex thing?

DANG. No!

GIRL. Well how's he gonna help?

DANG. I just have this feeling.

> *(Beat.)*

Where are your brochures?

GIRL. I got fired.

DANG. Oh I didn't realize it was a job-job.

GIRL. It wasn't. It was volunteer. I got fired from my volunteer job. Which is, like, so awesome.

DANG. Sorry.

GIRL. Yeah.

> *(Pause.)*

DANG. Why?

GIRL. Huh?

DANG. Why'd you get fired?

GIRL. Apparently my Korean isn't good enough. For a job for which *I don't get paid*. They said no one could understand what I was saying and it was a waste of the organization's limited supply of brochures.

> *(Beat.)*

DANG. Sucks.

GIRL. Everything's gone wacko with this Kim Jong Il thing anyway. No one's listening.

DANG. Fuckin' world.

GIRL. Yeah.

> *(Beat.)*

So you're just waiting here?

> (**DANG** *nods.*)

DANG. What are *you* gonna do?

GIRL. I don't know. But I was walking around all morning when I saw a magpie perched on the entrance to the subway – which according to the Eastern semiology class I took junior year means good news.

> (**DANG** *looks at her – "huh?"*)

> (*She takes out her phone and shows him a picture.*)

I saw this bird and figured if I rode the train awhile the answer would come to me.

DANG. You superstitious?

GIRL. No.

DANG. Then why?

> (**GIRL** *considers. Doesn't have a really good answer. So:*)

GIRL. Gotta believe in something.

> (*Beat.*)

Mind if I wait with you?

> (**DANG** *shakes his head. They ride.*)

3a.

(**MOTHER** *in the DMZ.*)

(*The* **GHOST OF KIM JONG IL** *enters.*)

GHOST. Hello.

MOTHER. *(Not believing her eyes.)* Kim Jong Il?

GHOST. Don't be scared.

MOTHER. I'm not.

GHOST. I'm not real, you know.

MOTHER. I know.

GHOST. *(Disappointed.)* How could you tell?

MOTHER. Because you're dead.

GHOST. True. That's true.

MOTHER. Why are you here?

GHOST. I'm looking for my father.

MOTHER. Here?

GHOST. Where else?

(**MOTHER** *opens her mouth to answer. But.*)

MOTHER. Okay.

GHOST. You?

MOTHER. I tripped on a rock while trying to jump off the roof of my condo.

GHOST. Ouchie.

(**MOTHER** *looks at him – "Ouchie?"*)

Do I have something in my teeth?

MOTHER. You were personally responsible for the starvation, torture, and death of millions of people.

I'm experiencing some cognitive dissonance.

GHOST. Would you like a button?

(*He unpins the red button [with his face on it] and offers it to her.*)

MOTHER. No thanks. I'm not really a fan.

GHOST. I did the best I could.

Things always seem so easy in the beginning.
But it's messy in the middle.
Getting through the middle is messy.

3b.

(...*In the hospital*, **HANNAH** *looks at the note.*)

GRANDMA'S VOICE. 까치야 –

(*Ding!*)

(**MOTHER** *appears, a memory.*)

MOTHER. "She sent it to you?"

HANNAH. Why? And why did you take it before you jumped?

MOTHER. "It was for me."

HANNAH. *I don't understand.*

MOTHER. "Hahahaha! That is very sad. I am sad. I want to die."

(**MOTHER** *looks at* **HANNAH.**)

(*Ding!*)

(**MOTHER** *disappears.*)

(**HANNAH** *looks at the bottle, then us.*)

HANNAH. Thirty-six hours, thirteen minutes, twelve seconds and counting –

3c.

(The DMZ.)

*(**MOTHER** still has the bloody weasel-rabbit foot in one hand.)*

*(The **GHOST OF KIM JONG IL** is seated, listening.)*

MOTHER. She only talked about two things: Not liking it there. And sweet potatoes. She sang this song:

I AMMMMMMMM A SWEET POTATO WOMANNNNNNN.
I SIIIIIT BELOW THE EARTH ANNNNNND –
ROOOT, ROOOOOOT, ROOOOT.

But she wouldn't eat. So that day.

I had baked it. Wrapped it in tin foil and pricked the foil with a fork to let the steam out. Like she used to do in winter when I was small. Wrapped it in a towel to keep it warm.

She was sleeping when I got there. So I sat. And I slept. Slept beside her.

She woke up screaming.

Mom? It's me. Do you know me?

I brought you something, I said.

"*Cold,*" she said. "*Cold!*" And slapped me.

I slapped her back.

I'd never. Before.

But for a second...*she saw me.*

"*I want to give you something,*" she said.

"*It's been in the family for a long time.*"

And she reached into the toe of her pink slipper, and pulled out a rock.

*(**HANNAH** appears, dimly, still in the hospital.)*

(She shakes the bottle gently.)

MOTHER.	HANNAH.
"*It's a wish*," she said. And she started to tell me a story, from my childhood, about a tiger, and a bear, in darkness for a hundred days –	"*It's a wish.*"

You have to *eat*, Mom.
My wish is for you to eat.
You have to eat.

"TAKE IT," she screamed.
"TAKE IT TAKE IT I
SAVED IT FOR YOU
TAKE IT TAKE IT TAKE
IT."

So I left.
And she jumped.   And she jumped.

        (*The* **GHOST OF KIM**   (**HANNAH** *puts the*
        JONG IL *nods.*)   *stone back in the*
                                          bottle.)
                                          (*Disappears.*)

MOTHER. I can't believe I'm telling you this.

GHOST. Why?

MOTHER. Because you're you.

GHOST. But I'm not *really* me, you know?

MOTHER. Still.

GHOST. And you needed to tell someone.

        (*The* **GHOST OF KIM JONG IL** *stands and dusts
        off his bottom.*)

MOTHER. You're going?

GHOST. Have to keep looking.

(He straightens his uniform.)

You're sure you don't want a button?

MOTHER. Er – no. Thank you though. You're a surprisingly good listener.

(Somewhere off, a roar.)

*(**MOTHER** turns toward the sound.)*

GHOST. She's old.

But best be careful.

It's weird here, you know?

(Shift.)

*(...In the hospital, **HANNAH** looks at the bottle.)*

HANNAH. "It's been in the family for a long time..."

(She closes her eyes. The flutter of a bird, getting closer.)

*(Somewhere in the past, **GRANDMA** appears, holding a bundled baby in her arms. **GRANDMA** clucks/tut-tuts, echoing the sound of a bird.)*

GRANDMA. "한나"

That's your name.

Like "하나" which means "one."

Because you're the first. The first to be born so far away.

(The baby cries.)

까치야 –

*(She clucks again. **HANNAH** approaches the memory, unseen.)*

Don't cry.

Don't cry little magpie.

We're all of us far from home.

*(**GRANDMA** takes something out of her pocket – a bottle with a small white stone.)*

*(She shakes it gently – a tiny rattling sound.
The baby quiets.)*

GRANDMA. It's a wish. It's been in the family for a long time.

*(**GRANDMA** leans closer.)*

"A long, long time ago, before there was a country to
have a name –"

*(The flutter of a bird departing. **GRANDMA**
disappears.)*

*(**HANNAH**, alone in the hospital, opens her
eyes.)*

4.

(The lobby of the Undersecretary of Defense.)

*(**FATHER** enters, exhausted and still wearing a bicycle helmet.)*

*(The **OFFICIAL** looks up.)*

*(**FATHER** makes the universal gesture for "jump off a tall building.")*

*(**OFFICIAL** looks at him – a suspended beat of absolutely zero recognition.)*

FATHER. *(Frustrated.)* [*North Korea!*]
   북한!

OFFICIAL. [*North Korea?!* What about *North Korea*?]
   북한?! 북한이 어쨌다고?

   *(**FATHER** has an idea.)*

FATHER. [*The secret tunnels.*]
   땅굴.

   (He makes the universal gesture for "secret underground tunnels.")

   [I have information. But only for Mr. Kwon.]
   하지만 권선생께서만 알려줄 수 있습니다.

   *(The **OFFICIAL** eyes him –)*

   (Beat.)

   *(– Then indicates he may go through. **FATHER** exits, as the **OFFICIAL** transforms –)*

5.

(*Ding-dong.*)

(*The* **OLD MAN IN COAT** *enters the subway car where* **DANG** *and* **GIRL** *sit.*)

DANG. Hey – HEY!

OLD MAN. (*In Korean.*) [Yes?]
예?

DANG. It's you!

OLD MAN. (*Confused.*) [Do I know you?]
전에 만난적이 있나요?

DANG. It's me!

OLD MAN. [Do you know me?]
저를 아십니까?

　　　　(**DANG** *grabs him by his coat.*)

GIRL. Hey –

DANG. It's me, remember?

GIRL. Are you sure –

OLD MAN. [Please, let go.]
제발 놔주세요.

DANG. Yes!

OLD MAN. [You're hurting me –]
아픕니다 –

GIRL. Maybe it's –

OLD MAN. [Please –]
제발 –

GIRL. – He says you're hurting him –

　　　　(**DANG** *lets go.*)

DANG. Oh. Oh hey, sorry man. I thought – I thought you were someone else.

　　　　(*The* **OLD MAN** *gets up, dazed.*)

　　　　(*Ding-dong.*)

(The doors open.)

(The **OLD MAN** *exits.)*

(He turns and looks back at **DANG***. He makes a tiger "rar" gesture.)*

(The doors close.)

Hey! *HEY!*

> (**DANG** *pounds on the door. As the car pulls away – lights flickering – the* **OLD MAN** *waves, then transforms as –)*

> *(The sound of a flutter again, this time followed by a caw.)*

> (**HANNAH** *looks up from the wish and sees the* **NURSE** *walking through –)*

HANNAH. Did you hear –

> *(The* **NURSE** *roars.)*

> (**HANNAH** *jumps back, watching as the* **NURSE** *transforms into –)*

6.

> (**UNDERSECRETARY OF DEFENSE KWON**, *a low-level Very Important Official, in his office.*)
>
> (**HANNAH** *has remained present throughout the preceding transition and watches from the periphery.*)
>
> (*The hum of flickering fluorescent lights.*)

KWON. [I understand you have information about the *tunnels* to *North Korea.*]
복한의 땅굴에 관한 정보를 가지고 있다고 들었는데, 맞습니까?

FATHER. [...Not me, my –]
제가 아니고, 저의 –

> (**KWON** *looks at* **HANNAH** *and snaps his fingers. The lights cease their flickering – suddenly, she [and we] now understand as the scene plays out in English:*)

– wife's mother – she lived in the *Sunrise Dewdrop Apartment City* for –

KWON. (*Hand over his heart.*) A brilliant project! We'll show those Communists! She is the source of this information, then?

FATHER. She's disappeared, you see –

KWON. Treason! Has she ever shown anti-democratic tendencies before?

FATHER. What –? No –

KWON. What was her place of origin?

FATHER. Huh?

KWON. Where was she *born*, man?

FATHER. Somewhere up north...her father was a farmer, they grew sweet potatoes.

KWON. So she's fled back to her traitorous roots, has she? Don't worry, we'll find her – no spy is safe!

FATHER. She's not a spy –

KWON. Then how did she have information about the *tunnels*?

FATHER. She's dead!

KWON. Dead!

How do you know she's dead?

FATHER. She jumped off the roof of a sixty-three-story building.

KWON. That's nothing to a spy!

FATHER. She wasn't a spy!

KWON. She came from the North!

FATHER. She was eighty years old –

KWON. That's like twenty in spy years!

FATHER. I need your help to recover her *body* –

KWON. Oh, we'll find her. Find her, arrest her, and have her brought up on charges! Get that information about the tunnels!

FATHER. But you'll go in and look for her?

(**KWON** *laughs.*)

KWON. Oh we can't go in.

FATHER. But you said –

KWON. We'll be waiting for her at the border when she comes out. But we can't go *in*. We'd trigger World War III!

FATHER. But she won't come out, she's probably dead –

KWON. Serves her right!

If she is dead, she's probably been devoured by tigers or bears already. The whole place is a wild animal park. Feral.

(*He makes a tiger "rar" gesture.*)

Dangerous.

FATHER. But –

7.

(The subway.)

GIRL. We should start a band.

DANG. Maybe.

GIRL. I'm serious.

DANG. I dunno how long I'll be here even.

GIRL. Well when do you have to be back in the States?

*(**DANG** shrugs.)*

So you don't actually *need* to be anywhere right now.

DANG. Well I can't stay here.

GIRL. Why not?

DANG. It's just – different you know?

GIRL. Duh.

DANG. I don't speak the language.

GIRL. So learn.

DANG. I'm American.

GIRL. So?

DANG. It doesn't bother you? That everyone here looks like you?

GIRL. Says who?

DANG. Everyone's the same. The same hair color the same height the same...

GIRL. *(A reminder.)* Racist.

DANG. I don't mean exactly the –
Like we're all related. Like I walk down the street back home and see white people, black people, fat people – and I know I'm me because I'm *not* them. Here any one of these people could be me, some bizarro version of me, cousins and uncles and aunts I've never met before. It's claustrophobic. Besides, who knows what's gonna happen with this whole North Korea thing. Maybe the whole place goes up in a mushroom cloud. I don't wanna be here when it does.

(Ding-dong.)

(The **OLD MAN IN COAT** *enters the subway.)*

(Ding-dong.)

GIRL. Hey. Hey.

(She nudges him. He looks over.)

DANG. Oh shit.

(He looks again.)

Maybe?

Shit.

GIRL. So ask.

DANG. But what if –

*(***GIRL*** stands up and approaches the* **OLD MAN.***)*

GIRL. *(In terrible Korean.)* [Excuse me? Excuse?]
Shill-eh-ham-nee-dah.

OLD MAN. [Yes?]
예?

GIRL. [Do you this man young know?]
All-ah ee-nam-jah huck-shee?

OLD MAN. *(Broken English.)* You Korean terrible.

GIRL. [I know.]
All-ah.

OLD MAN. [You should really know your own language better.]
모국어는 좀더 잘알아야 할것 같아요.

GIRL. [*I know.* Do you this man young know?]
All-ah. All-ah ee-nam-jah huck-shee?

(The **OLD MAN** *peers at* **DANG.***)*

OLD MAN. [I'm not sure. Have we met before?]
모르겠는데. 전에 만난적 있나요?

*(***DANG*** freezes, terrified.)*

DANG. What'dhe say?

GIRL. He asked if you've cartooned before. That can't be right.

OLD MAN. <u>만난</u>적.

GIRL. Met. Met.

DANG. I think so.

GIRL. [He think maybe.]
   Ah-mah-do.

OLD MAN. [In that case then okay.]
   그렇다면 나도 어쩌면.

GIRL. He says okay.

DANG. Okay?

OLD MAN. Okay.

DANG. What does that mean?

GIRL. [What does that –]
   Juh-geh-moo-sun –

>   (*The* **OLD MAN** *takes* **DANG***'s face in his hands.*)

OLD MAN. (*In English.*) You...very sad... I sorry for...you sad.

>   (*Suddenly, he smiles.*)

[Here:]
자:

>   (*He reaches into his pocket and pulls out a small object.*)

For you.

>   (*He presses the object into* **DANG***'s hands.*)
>   (*Ding-dong.*)
>   (*The* **OLD MAN** *exits.*)
>   (*Ding-dong.*)

GIRL. What is it?

>   (**DANG** *opens his hands and shows her a small clump of garlic.*)

(Shift.)

(...In the hospital, **HANNAH** *holds the bottle.)*

(Shakes it gently.)

(Gets an idea.)

(She looks around her – left, right.)

(Clutching the bottle tightly, she closes her eyes. Whispers:)

HANNAH. I wish she would wake up.

(She opens her eyes.)

(Looks around her – only hospital sounds. Nothing has changed.)

(To herself.) Stupid.

(She curls up on the bench, defeated.)

(And goes to sleep. As she dreams –)

8.

(**GRANDMOTHER TIGER** *enters the DMZ. She is a spry, skinny thing in a nightgown and the same pink slippers we saw in Part I. She looks just like a grandmother would, but with the paws of a tiger.*)

(*She picks her teeth with the pin of a button of* **KIM JONG IL.**)

GRANDMOTHER TIGER. Hello.

MOTHER. Hello.

GRANDMOTHER TIGER. I'm here to eat you.

MOTHER. Oh.

GRANDMOTHER TIGER. I had worked out this whole elaborate disguise to get through the door of your cottage. But you don't have a door-of-your-cottage.

MOTHER. No.

GRANDMOTHER TIGER. You don't have a cottage at all.

MOTHER. No.

GRANDMOTHER TIGER. All that work. I could have sworn you'd have a cottage.

(*She scratches her head.*)

I'm getting old.

MOTHER. It's a very good disguise.

GRANDMOTHER TIGER. Thank you.

MOTHER. Except for the paws.

(**GRANDMOTHER TIGER** *looks down at her paws.*)

GRANDMOTHER TIGER. I knew I forgot something. Getting old is a terrible thing.

(*She tosses the pin behind her.*)

You're sure you don't have a cottage? Somewhere?

MOTHER. I have a condo…

GRANDMOTHER TIGER. What's that?

MOTHER. Like a cottage. But taller.

GRANDMOTHER TIGER. Two stories?

MOTHER. Taller.

GRANDMOTHER TIGER. Three?

MOTHER. Taller.

GRANDMOTHER TIGER. What is the world coming to?

MOTHER. Where did you get those slippers?

> (**GRANDMOTHER TIGER** *looks down.*)

GRANDMOTHER TIGER. Huh. Not sure.

> (*She stretches her paws.*)

Oh well lunchtime.

> (*She steps toward* **MOTHER**.)

MOTHER. You don't *have* to eat me.

GRANDMOTHER TIGER. I have to *eat*.

MOTHER. Not *me*.

GRANDMOTHER TIGER. Who then?

MOTHER. Or you could wait. I'm not going anywhere.

GRANDMOTHER TIGER. That's what they all say.

MOTHER. I can't. The landmines?

> (*She makes the universal gesture for* "landmines-then-boom.")

GRANDMOTHER TIGER. True.

> (**GRANDMOTHER TIGER** *steps toward* **MOTHER**, *sniffs.*)

Alright. I could use a little digestion time. Work up an appetite.

> (*She starts to stretch and do some calisthenics.*)
>
> (*Maybe she hums a tune, which sounds suspiciously like "Sweet Potato Woman."*)

MOTHER. Where are we?

> (**GRANDMOTHER TIGER** *shrugs.*)

GRANDMOTHER TIGER. You know.

MOTHER. But how did I get here.

>   (**GRANDMOTHER TIGER** *shrugs again.*)

How did you get here?

GRANDMOTHER TIGER. Oh I've always been here.
There's not a lot of it left anymore.
But this is my home.

MOTHER. God, you look just like her.

GRANDMOTHER TIGER. Don't I though.

>   (*Beat.*)

Who?

9.

(**HANNAH** *wakes up in the hospital.*)

(**FATHER** *is seated next to her, holding his bicycle helmet.*)

HANNAH. Mom?

(*She rubs her eyes.*)

(*Beat.*)

You were right. I never should have shown her the note.

(*She looks at the bottle.*)

But it wasn't just the note. It was this. I don't *understand* – why did Grandma want me to have this?

FATHER. (*Looking at the wish.*) Do you think it's real? Maybe if I hold it –

(*She instinctively pulls the bottle back, the tiniest bit.*)

(*Beat.*)

(*She hands him the bottle.*)

(*He closes his eyes.*)

"I wish..."

(*He opens his eyes.*)

(*Silence.*)

(*Nothing.*)

Do you know how I met your mother?

(**HANNAH** *shakes her head.*)

Because of my father.

HANNAH. I thought he died when you were a kid.

FATHER. He did. But before I was born, when he lived in the North – he was a cyclist. A good one. He was going to be in the Olympics! He was training when the war broke out.

HANNAH. Oh. Wow.

FATHER. But the North didn't have a team. So he got on his bike and rode south.

He left *everyone* – rode and rode until he reached the front...and got shot in the leg while crossing.

So I never had a bicycle. Too sad. And no one had cars, it was all by bicycle, so I was *always* late. On the first day of school 1973 I was *twenty minutes* late and the teacher had already locked the door. I called out "Hello? Professor, I'm sorry it will never happen again." And I knocked, and no one answered, and I knocked again, and no one answered, and I cursed my father and his bicycle and myself for never learning how to ride when suddenly the most beautiful girl I'd ever seen opened the door.

And all of it – the long ride, the gunshot, my lifetime of lateness – it all made sense. In the end.

We have to keep going.

HANNAH. There's nowhere to go. We can't *do* anything.

FATHER. WELL WE CAN'T JUST SIT HERE.

> *(Beat.)*

Sorry.

I.

Sorry.

> *(He stands.)*

I'll be back soon.

HANNAH. Where are you –

> *(The phone rings.)*

> (**FATHER** *exits as* **DANG** *enters, holding his hat.)*

> *(The phone rings.)*

DANG. Where's Dad going?

> *(The phone rings.)*

> (**HANNAH** *grabs the phone and hits "ignore." It's maybe a little violent.)*

HANNAH. (Christ Teddy.)

DANG. Does he even know you're here?

HANNAH. *(Part to* **DANG***, part to herself.)* I've spent my whole life studying, to make something of myself, and I'm not going to do what Mom did, I'm not going to give that up to stay some housewife in Argentina.

> *(She spins around.)*

Where have you been?!

DANG. You ever hear this story, about a bear and a tiger?

HANNAH. No – can I see the video?

DANG. Huh?

HANNAH. The video. Can I see it?

> *(He takes out his phone and presses a few buttons.)*
>
> *(A* **WOMAN** *walks through a door, her back to us. She looks out. Breathes in.)*
>
> *(Suddenly, she runs. She spreads her arms – and freezes, feet flexed, knees bent.* **DANG** *hits the phone. Jiggles it.)*

DANG. Buffering. Piece of shit.

> *(He shakes it again. No change.)*

HANNAH. She doesn't seem sad.

> *(Beat.)*

Or scared. She doesn't look like she's running away from something.

DANG. Then why would she jump.

> *(***HANNAH** *looks at the wish. She grabs her coat.)*

HANNAH. Come on.

DANG. But what if –?

HANNAH. Dad'll be back any minute.

> *(***HANNAH** *pockets the bottle.)*

HANNAH. Call him on the way.

DANG. The way where?

(They exit as –)

(Somewhere else, **FATHER** *pedals furiously toward home.)*

10.

(The roof of the Sunrise Dewdrop Apartment City for Senior Living. Cold.)

(DANG and HANNAH are bundled up in coats and hats. They stare down.)

DANG. How many floors?

HANNAH. Sixty-three.

(They look across the DMZ.)

DANG. It's pretty.

HANNAH. Weird, right?

DANG. Quiet.

HANNAH. Grass.

DANG. Trees.

HANNAH. The whole world used to look like this.

DANG. Minus the mines.

HANNAH. You can't see the mines. That's like the point of mines.

(HANNAH steps toward the edge.)

DANG. Han?

(HANNAH closes her eyes and reaches her arms out like the woman in the video.)

HANNAH. This is what we do, right? The women in our family?

DANG. Han, you're freaking me out.

HANNAH. We throw ourselves off high buildings?

DANG. Seriously, Han –

(A warning shot. DANG squints across the DMZ.)

Hey – was that –

HANNAH. *(Eyes still closed.)* Yeah.

DANG. Those dudes have *guns*?

HANNAH. Sounds like it.

DANG. Can they see us?

HANNAH. The woman downstairs said don't make any sudden movements.

DANG. Whatthefuck, Han?!?

HANNAH. (At least I think that's what she said.)

DANG. We could get shot!

HANNAH. Nothing'll happen.

DANG. How do you know?

HANNAH. This thing's been going on for fifty years.

(She opens her eyes.)

HEY! HEY YOU OVER THERE!

DANG. Are you crazy?

HANNAH. YOU WITH THE GUNS!

DANG. Stop it you're going to get us killed!

HANNAH. OVER HERE!

(She waves.)

WHY DON'T YOU DO SOMETHING ALREADY!

*(**DANG** tries to pull **HANNAH** back.)*

(Far off, but not too far, a warning shot is fired.)

YEAH THAT'S RIGHT, CAN'T CAN YOU?

(Another warning shot.)

DANG. They don't speak ENGLISH Hannah.

HANNAH. WHY DON'T YOU SPEAK ENGLISH YOU COMMUNIST MOTHERFUCKERS!

(Another warning shot.)

DANG. Because they're Korean.

HANNAH. I'm Korean and I speak English.

DANG. But you don't speak Korean.

HANNAH. I COULD IF I WANTED TO.

(She looks around for something to throw. There isn't anything [it's a rooftop], so she takes off a shoe and hurls it off the roof.)

HEY! HEY YOU!

(She takes off the other shoe, throws it.)

OVER HERE!

DANG. Are you trying to start World War III?

*(***HANNAH*** *takes out the bottle and leans her arm back –)*

No!

*(***DANG*** *grabs her arm.)*

(They struggle.)

HANNAH. It's mine I can do what I –

DANG. *– Stop –*

HANNAH. It's just a stupid rock in a –

(She wrests the bottle away from him...)

(...And hurls it off the rooftop.)

HAAAAAAAAAAAAAAAAAAAA!

(They watch it arc up, then down, then –)

DANG. Whoa! Did you see that?

HANNAH. *(Still looking.)* It caught it.

DANG. That bird is the *shit*.

HANNAH. Shitty bird.

DANG. Yo bird! You are the motherfuckin' shit!

(They watch the bird.)

HANNAH. Fuck. Fuckettyfuckfuckfuckfuckfuck. *Fuck.*

DANG. It's coming back!

HANNAH. Huh?

DANG. Duck!

(The bird swoops over them and drops the bottle on **HANNAH***'s head.)*

HANNAH. Ow!

DANG. Do it again!

HANNAH. No.

(Before she can react, he grabs the bottle and hurls it across the roof.)

HANNAH. Dang!

(They watch. The bird catches it again. Starts to come back again.)

DANG. Holy shit!

*(**HANNAH** ducks behind him, trying to protect her head. She zigs. It zigs. She zags. It zags.)*

(Finally, it flies away.)

HANNAH. Ha!

*(The bottle launches at **HANNAH**'s head.)*

(This time, she catches it.)

It threw it.

DANG. YEAH!

HANNAH. That shitty bird threw this at me.

DANG. I think it's a magpie.

HANNAH. That's what she called me – "little magpie."

DANG. *Magpie* – that means good news, yo!

HANNAH. Says who?

DANG. This girl.

HANNAH. What girl?

DANG. Just a girl. She said it's good.

HANNAH. *(Skeptical.)* 'Cause she's some kind of expert?

DANG. 'Cause sometimes you're not the only one who knows shit and making other people feel dumb doesn't make you smart and *you never listen and you're not even wearing shoes*!

(Beat.)

HANNAH. Whoa. Sorry.

DANG. I had to ask Mom and Dad Grandma's first name. That's fucked up, right? How do you not know something like that?

HANNAH. It's not really a first-name-basis-for-old-people kind of country.

> *(Beat.)*

What was it?

DANG. DaHee.

DaHwee?

Shit.

> *(Beat.)*

> *(They look at the bird in the distance.)*

HANNAH. "Little Magpie"... It means good news?

> (**DANG** *nods.*)

> (**HANNAH** *offers him the bottle.*)

She should have sent it to you.

> (**DANG** *shakes his head. Hands it back.*)

DANG. She sent it to you for a reason.

HANNAH. How do you know?

> *(He shrugs.)*

DANG. Gotta believe in something, right?

HANNAH. Mom said it was for her.

> *(She looks at him.)*

Give me your hand.

> *(He does. She puts the bottle in it, so that they are holding it together. They close their eyes.)*

I wish –

DANG. I wish –

HANNAH. One –

DANG. Two?

HANNAH & DANG. Three!

> *(They open their eyes and launch the bottle. A loud squawk.)*

HANNAH. OhmygodIthinkwekilledit.

(They watch.)

DANG. Nah. Nah, it's okay. And it's got it, see?

(They watch it fly far, far away.)

*(**HANNAH** turns to **DANG**.)*

HANNAH. You look different. Why do you look different?

(He shrugs.)

DANG. Long story.

(Beat.)

HANNAH. Okay.

DANG. Okay what.

HANNAH. I'm listening.

*(**DANG** takes his hat out of his pocket. He holds it out to **HANNAH**, bottom-up, indicating she should reach inside. She pulls out the clump of garlic. She looks at him, a question.)*

*(**DANG** puts the knit hat on his head, tugs it over his ears. [Chronologically, we have arrived at the same moment his story began in Part II – Arrival.])*

DANG. When I get to the city it is like so fuckin' *crowded*, more crowded than anyplace I've ever been and just so full of like *Asian* people, you know?

11.

> (*The DMZ.*)
>
> (*The shadow of a magpie overhead.*)
>
> (*An object lands on* **MOTHER***'s head – plop.*)

MOTHER. Ow.

> (**MOTHER** *picks up the bottle and looks up. The bird is nowhere in sight.*)

GRANDMOTHER TIGER. What's that?

> (**MOTHER** *shakes the bottle gently. A tiny rattling sound.*)

MOTHER. "It's a wish."

GRANDMOTHER TIGER. (*Skeptical.*) It looks like a rock.

> (**GRANDMOTHER** *gets closer.*)
>
> (**MOTHER** *takes the stone out of the bottle.*)
>
> (**GRANDMOTHER** *sniffs, curious.*)
>
> (*Then gets closer, closer...and suddenly* roars, *retreating.*)

GRANDMOTHER. TAKE IT AWAY!

MOTHER. (*Holding it toward her.*) Please.

GRANDMOTHER. (*Retreating.*) TAKE IT TAKE IT TAKE IT TAKE IT!

> (**MOTHER** *puts the bottle in her pocket.*)
>
> (**GRANDMOTHER** *falls silent, then circles* **MOTHER**, *assessing the threat.*)

MOTHER. Do you know me?

> (**GRANDMOTHER** *sniffs toward* **MOTHER**.)

GRANDMOTHER. You remind me of –

MOTHER. Yes?

GRANDMOTHER. Someone. From before.

MOTHER. Who?

GRANDMOTHER. It hurts.

(She shudders.)

GRANDMOTHER. The forgetting.

MOTHER. Hurts how?

> *(She puts her hand gently on* **GRANDMOTHER***'s paw.)*

Please.

> **(GRANDMOTHER** *squeezes her eyes shut.)*
>
> *(The light becomes a little less bright.)*

GRANDMOTHER. Like a tunnel that goes on forever.

> **(GRANDMOTHER** *squeezes her eyes tighter.)*
>
> *(The light becomes even less bright.)*

Dark.

MOTHER. Cold?

GRANDMOTHER. No light.

No light at all.

> *(Beat.)*

I didn't like it there.

MOTHER. Where?

GRANDMOTHER. The waiting.

MOTHER. Where –

> *(Far, far away – a muffled, rumbling, animal sound echoes somewhere cold and damp. Or is it thunder?)*

GRANDMOTHER. There's someone sleeping beside me.

And the smell. God –

MOTHER. Do you know me?

GRANDMOTHER. – *The smell.*

MOTHER. The smell of –?

GRANDMOTHER. Rot –

Root –

MOTHER. *(Sharp.)* Root –?

GRANDMOTHER. Rotting –

MOTHER. Do you know me?

GRANDMOTHER. *(Looking at an invisible someone on the ground.)* Do I know him?

MOTHER. *Her* –

GRANDMOTHER. *(To herself.)* Did I dream it?

MOTHER. – No –

GRANDMOTHER. Did I dream it all?

MOTHER. No –

GRANDMOTHER. *(Clutching her head.)* Going – All going – One hundred days...

MOTHER. One hundred –

GRANDMOTHER. I promised him to –

MOTHER & GRANDMOTHER. Stay.

GRANDMOTHER. But I wish –

MOTHER. I wish –

GRANDMOTHER. I miss –

MOTHER. I *need* –

GRANDMOTHER. Birds –

 Trees –

MOTHER. Please –

GRANDMOTHER. – *There* –

 Before I forget –

MOTHER. If you waited –

GRANDMOTHER. *(To herself.)* You could wait –

MOTHER. Can you wait –

GRANDMOTHER. No.

MOTHER. – You could stay –

GRANDMOTHER. Or –

MOTHER. Or –

GRANDMOTHER. Or –

MOTHER & GRANDMOTHER. – *You could fly.*

 (The world goes silent.)

 *(**GRANDMOTHER** looks out, remembering. Then shrugs.)*

GRANDMOTHER. Maybe I was tired.

Maybe I was crazy.

Maybe I missed my home.

MOTHER. Who are you?

GRANDMOTHER. I don't remember. But I'm the last.

Beginning, middle, end.

> (**GRANDMOTHER** *is now very, very close to* **MOTHER.**)
>
> (*And perhaps for a moment – the light – recognition –*)
>
> (*She touches the stone.*)

Tell me.

Tell me the story of this.

MOTHER. Will you let me go?

GRANDMOTHER. Yes.

MOTHER. And the landmines?

GRANDMOTHER. There might be. A way.

> (**MOTHER** *presses the stone gently into* **GRANDMOTHER**'s *paw.*)

MOTHER. I think.

I think it was for you.

12a.

(The hospital.)

*(**HANNAH** and **DANG** wait.)*

*(**FATHER** enters, dragging a leafy trellis behind him.)*

FATHER. It's an outside-outside wall.

DANG. Inside.

(They help him prop it up. Maybe sit on the ground to keep it steady.)

HANNAH. What was her name? Mom's mom.

FATHER. Da Hee.

DANG. How did that never come up?

FATHER. It's not really a first-name-basis-for-old-people kind of country.

HANNAH. Still.

FATHER. And you never asked.

*(**DANG** shows him the clump of garlic.)*

DANG. Does this mean something to you?

*(**FATHER** breaks open the clump. He gives them each a small clove.)*

FATHER. Endurance. Good for you.

(They peel back the skin and chew.)

DANG. *(Chewing.)* Oh man [this is disgusting.]

(They swallow.)

HANNAH. What did Grandma do? Before she came here. Before the war.

FATHER. I don't know. Your mother might.

DANG. We'll ask her when she wakes up, then.

FATHER. When she wakes up.

HANNAH. When she wakes up.

12b.

(A giant explosion. As the rubble clears, we see...)

(...A secret tunnel under the DMZ.)

*(**MOTHER** climbs down.)*

MOTHER. *(Calling up.)* I've heard about these tunnels!

(She looks in both directions.)

Which way?

(No answer.)

Which way is south?!

(No answer.)

(Silence. Then a giggle.)

WHICH WAY AM I SUPPOSED TO GO?

(The giggle gets farther away.)

(Farther.)

(Farther.)

(No answer. She is alone.)

(She hits the wall [ow], then nurses her hand.)

Fine.

(She closes her eyes and spins. Walks into a wall.)

Ow.

(She turns left, and goes.)

12c.

> *(The hospital.)*
>
> **(FATHER, HANNAH,** *and* **DANG** *asleep against the propped-up trellis.)*
>
> **(GIRL** *sits next to* **DANG,** *sipping a cup of coffee.)*
>
> *(A* **NURSE** *enters.)*

NURSE. [Are you the *Lees*?]
혹시 이씨 가족입니까?

> **(GIRL** *nudges* **DANG.)**

GIRL. Hey.

> **(DANG** *mumbles in his sleep and puts his head on* **GIRL's** *shoulder.)*

Is your last name Lee?

> **(GIRL** *shakes* **DANG** *gently, which shakes* **HANNAH,** *which shakes* **FATHER.)**

Hey –

> **(FATHER** *wakes up.)*

NURSE. [Are you the *Lees*?]
이씨 가족입니까?

> *(He jumps up. But:)*

FATHER. [Which *Lees*?]
어느 이씨 가족 말씀입니까?

> *(She double-checks the clipboard.)*

NURSE. [Mr. *Lee ho-sun*?]
이호선씨?

FATHER. [Yes!]
예!

> *(She smiles. Indicates they may go in now.)*
>
> **(FATHER, DANG,** *and* **GIRL** *exit.)*

(**HANNAH** *lingers – there's something familiar about this* **NURSE**, *too. Like a distant memory.*)

(*The* **NURSE** *returns* **HANNAH**'s *gaze. Without breaking eye contact, the* **NURSE** *removes her costume, folding it gently over her arm.*)

(*She gives* **HANNAH** *a tiny nod – then exits.*)

(**HANNAH** *looks at us.*)

HANNAH. This is the story of a wish.

(**HANNAH** *steps forward into –*)

PART V. THE END.

HANNAH. Beginning, middle...end.

Did the beginning cause the middle, or the middle the end? Or did they just...happen?

(Beat.)

It's time to wrap up what's left of our story. This is the part between the middle and the end, or "denouement" – That's French, for "untying."

What happened to Grandma is still a mystery. But her wish...brought me home. And maybe...

(She stops herself. Shakes her head.)

In any event, Mom is awake and safe, Grandma is gone or dead or both. My father will probably not give up, but for now is riding his bike back to the university. My brother is staying here and maybe, just maybe, has found a new band, and a girl. And as for me –

(The phone rings.)

(The phone rings.)

(She looks at it.)

(The phone –)

Teddy, hi.

I know.

I know.

I'm sorry.

I can't –

(She looks at us.)

I can't talk right now, okay?

(Pause.)

HANNAH. Tonight won't work.

I'm not there. I'm with my family in Korea.

> *(Beat.)*

Yes the country.

Well that's where I'm from.

That's where I am.

> *(Pause.)*

Teddy, I –

I can't live in Argentina.

I – I love you and I can't live in Argentina.

> *(Pause.)*

I don't know.

> *(Pause.)*

I'll be back in seventeen hours to take my boards, and then after that I want a long hot bath and one night of sleep and...we'll talk, okay? I'll tell you the whole story.

I have to go.

I have to finish.

> *(She looks at us, lowers her voice into the phone:)*

This thing. But I'll see you soon.

Yeah.

> *(Pause.)*

I know. Me too.

> *(She hangs up. Recomposes.)*

Okay where were we.

Momissafehermom,mybrother,myfatherisriding hisbike... And as for me –

> *(A boarding pass flutters down from the sky. She catches it.)*

I have a flight in exactly three hours from Incheon International Airport to JFK, where I will arrive just in time for Part One of my exam to become a board-certified pediatric neurologist. This – as my father will remind me at the airport with his usual pat on the shoulder, is –

HANNAH.	FATHER.
– A very important time for me.	– A very important time for you.
	*(**FATHER** passes **HANNAH** her suitcase, then exits.)*

And that's the end. Or, for you academic types –

> *(**MOTHER** enters.)*

MOTHER. Hannah?

HANNAH. Mom, what –

MOTHER. Come here.

HANNAH. I'm almost done.

MOTHER. Just a minute –

HANNAH. Where?

MOTHER. *Here.*

> *(**HANNAH** hesitates, but steps toward...)*
>
> *(...A rooftop gazebo, looking out over the city. A full vine of broad, heart-shaped sweet potato leaves spills down one lattice wall.)*

We're not there yet.

HANNAH. Where?

MOTHER. The end.

HANNAH. Where are we?

MOTHER. *(Duh.)* Gazebo.

> *(Pause.)*

Can you hear that?

> *(**HANNAH** tries to listen. Far, far below, city sounds begin to bloom – traffic, doors opening and closing, telephones, footsteps, the low murmur of a million voices.)*

HANNAH. It's noisy. This is a noisy city.

MOTHER. Listen.

> *(She does.)*
>
> *(The city sounds swell, circle, and melt together. Somewhere far [but not too far] – the wind moves through a grove of untouched, ancient trees. A tiger pads through the grass. Perhaps, over his-slash-her head is a tiny, stubborn bird.)*

HANNAH. Mom?

MOTHER. Yes?

> *(Beat.)*

HANNAH. Where did you get a gazebo?

MOTHER. Amishcountrygazebos.com.

What are you going to do about your young man?

HANNAH. I don't know.

MOTHER. That's okay, sometimes.

HANNAH. I don't like it.

MOTHER. That's because you're an obsessive control freak.

> *(Gently mocking, making the universal gesture for "three clearly separate parts that are subdivided neatly/comprehensibly":)*

"Beginning, middle, end."

So stiff.

You should maybe loosen up.

HANNAH. Thanks.

MOTHER. "That's French, for untying."

HANNAH. Okay.

> *(They look out, and listen, in silence.)*

Why do you think she did it?

> *(**MOTHER** is silent.)*

You know, I could stay.

MOTHER. You'll miss your test.

HANNAH. I don't want you to...you know.

> (**MOTHER** *looks at her, puzzled.*)

You know.

MOTHER. You mean –

> (*She makes the universal gesture for "jump off a tall building and splat."*)

HANNAH. Not funny.

MOTHER. Little funny.

> (*Silence.*)

Not even a little?

HANNAH. No.

> (*But she smiles.*)

MOTHER. Can I tell you a story?

HANNAH. Okay.

MOTHER. A long, long time ago, before there was a country to have a name, there was a tiger, and a bear.

HANNAH. I know this one.

MOTHER. Really?

HANNAH. The bear makes it but the tiger doesn't.

MOTHER. And then?

HANNAH. That's the end.

MOTHER. No.

HANNAH. No?

MOTHER. The bear, now a woman, married the king of heaven and gave birth to a boy, who ruled the world for a thousand years. And before she died, she told her son to burn her remains. He would find something, she said. Something in the ash – a gift. For an old friend. Find him alone in the deepest woods, at the base of the highest mountain. When he sees it, he'll know. He'll know that I am gone.

This is my last wish.

Her son built a huge fire, just as she had said, and when the flames died down – inside the ash was a stone. It was beautiful, this stone. Smooth and round and white as bone. He couldn't bear to part with it. So he placed it in his pocket, and told himself that someday, he would carry out her wish. Just not today. And before he died, he told his daughter the story. And she promised she would carry out the wish, someday. Just not today. And with each generation, the story grew fainter, until finally all that remained were three words –

> (**MOTHER** *takes out the bottle, now empty, from her pocket.*)

MOTHER & HANNAH. "It's a wish."

HANNAH. Not a genie –

MOTHER. Or a magic fish –

HANNAH. Or a severed monkey's paw –

MOTHER. Not the kind you make.

HANNAH. The kind you carry out.

MOTHER. A gift.

HANNAH. *(Looking at the bottle.)* It's empty. How did –

MOTHER. It's...complicated.

HANNAH. Is it true?

MOTHER. It's a story.

HANNAH. But was it *real*. Did it really –

MOTHER. "All memories are suspect, at the neural level."

> (*Despite herself,* **HANNAH** *laughs.*)

It's enough. Let it be enough.

HANNAH. You never talk about her.

MOTHER. She had a hard life. And you never asked.

HANNAH. I'm asking now.

MOTHER. Your plane.

HANNAH. Please.

> (*She sets down her suitcase.*)
> (**MOTHER** *looks out, then at her daughter.*)
> (*Inhales to speak, as –*)

(– Her **MOTHER** *appears, rushes forward, throws her arms wide open and leaps into –)*

(A blinding flash –)

End of Play*

---

*If there were a place in this play for a song, it would be here. Perhaps right before (or even instead of) a traditional curtain call. Homespun and celebratory. Full cast. If this were to happen, it might be performed as though giving an awesome post-play thank you gift to the audience. Or a ridiculous one. Or both. This song must be an original composition.

Hannah and the Dread Gazebo

Obadiah Eaves

Sweet Potato Woman